Unleashing the Potential of Artificial Intelligence in K-12 Education: Reimagining How Learning Happens

AI in K-12 Education

Adam Smith

Published by A. Smith Media, 2023.

UNLEASHING THE POTENTIAL OF ARTIFICIAL INTELLIGENCE IN K-12 EDUCATION: REIMAGINING HOW LEARNING HAPPENS

First edition. May 30, 2023.

ISBN: 979-8223933892

Written by Adam Smith.

Table of Contents

Chapter 1: "Unlocking the Potential of AI-Enhanced Adaptive Learning in K-12 Education"

The incorporation of artificial intelligence (AI) strategies within the educational realm has breathed life into an entirely new sector of the academic world, known as AI-Enhanced Adaptive Learning (DIAL). With K-12 education being the most prominent division of this advancement, there is an invaluable opportunity for it to offer an enormous amount of advantages which could, in turn, revolutionize how students learn. Through a combination of intelligent algorithms and adaptive learning technologies, DIAL is a process aimed at optimizing learning by utilizing data tracking and predictive analyses to personalize instruction, specifically tailored to what students need to learn.

At its heart, DIAL is an educational system which uses sophisticated algorithms and predictive analysis in order to craft individual learning paths, customized to the student's needs and preferences. This takes into account a student's previous knowledge, current performance, and desired outcome in order to provide the most effective tutoring possible. In a sense, DIAL has certain features that are reminiscent of a well-trained teacher, one who can recognize where students are and help guide them through more nuanced study and exploration.

One of the most important aspects of DIAL is its ability to structure learning in a way that can respond to an individual student's needs and diverse learning styles. For example, AI-generated personalized curriculum and tailored assignments for students based on their personal goals allow each student to learn at their own pace, resulting in a more individual and efficient learning experience. DIAL also gives teachers the ability to monitor the progress of individual students in real-time so that they can adjust instruction and challenges on the fly. In addition, AI-algorithms can also be used to predict what learning material will be most engaging and relevant to a student, which is essential for reliable educational outcomes.

Another significant benefit of DIAL is its ability to make decisions based on data. The ability to access large amounts of educational data and being able to analyze it precisely with AI algorithms not only gives educators the ability to see a comprehensive view of a student's academic development, but also provides them with better insights into their teaching abilities and satisfaction rates. This helps teachers identify the areas where it should be improved, as well as empowering them to make more strategic interventions when it comes to teaching.

As well as the advantages mentioned above, DIAL also provides an avenue for students to stay involved and connected. DIAL can be enabled with communication tools such as messaging systems and virtual help-desks, which students can use to contact teachers and peers at any time. In addition, DIAL can also be integrated with online portals and social networks, giving students the opportunity to enhance their learning journey with a variety of additional features and resources.

When it comes to unlocking the potential of AI-Enhanced Adaptive Learning in K-12 Education, the key is to make sure that the system is implemented properly and that it is optimized to meet the individual needs of each student. It is essential that stakeholders recognize and understand the value of DIAL and how it can boost the whole educational sector by providing personalized, up-to-date assistance and tools in supporting strong, effective educational outcomes. Ultimately, DIAL has the potential to completely revolutionize the way K-12 education functions, leading to a more effective, responsive, and tailored educational experience for all students.

Chapter 2: "Unlocking the Potential of AI-Powered Adaptive Learning for K12 Education"

Over the past few decades, the scope of artificial intelligence (AI) has grown immensely, to the point where it is now able to be used in a range of applications, from analyzing data to natural language processing to robotics. The potent combination of AI and machine learning has now made it possible for technology to be better applied in educational settings, particularly in the area of adaptive learning. Adaptive learning is a specific type of technology-enabled learning that responds in real time to the needs and preferences of individual learners. This type of learning has become a major focus in recent years, as it has the potential to be incredibly effective in meeting the diverse needs of K-12 students, allowing educators to ensure that no student is left behind.

AI-powered adaptive learning has the potential to revolutionize the way K-12 students are taught. Rather than relying on a one-size-fits-all approach, adaptive learning accommodates each student's individual learning needs. This allows educators to tailor content and activities in a way that will suit each student's needs, thus enabling them to engage with material more efficiently and productively. AI-powered adaptive learning traditionally works by using data-driven algorithms that analyze student information such as performance records, personal preferences, and even psychometric data, to determine the best educational path for each student. It then uses this data to generate personalized instruction plans, providing teachers with the tools to effectively engage with each student.

There are several potential benefits to using AI-powered adaptive learning in K-12 education. One of the most obvious benefits is that adaptive learning can provide students with personalized learning experiences. This means that students can learn at their own pace and focus on the topics that are most important to them. Additionally, adaptive learning can enable teachers to more quickly identify areas where students may be struggling and provide targeted help and guidance. This can help teachers to correct deficiencies before they worsen, resulting in improved academic performance.

AI-powered adaptive learning also has the potential to make education more accessible. By removing traditional barriers to education, AI-powered adaptive learning can make educational content available to students who previously may not have been able to access it. This could include students with disabilities, students in remote or rural locations, and students with fewer financial resources.

AI-powered adaptive learning can also help to improve the on the whole quality of education. As adaptive learning systems learn from the data they collect, they can identify trends within the educational environment that may need to be addressed. Furthermore, AI-powered adaptive learning systems can be used to identify potential areas for improvement and help teachers to better engage with their students.

Ultimately, AI-powered adaptive learning has the potential to dramatically improve the educational experience for K-12 students. By targeting individual student needs more effectively and providing teachers with the tools to better engage with all their students, AI-powered adaptive learning can help to ensure that no student is left behind. With continued advances in educational technology, AI-powered adaptive learning can help to create a more equal and effective learning environment for all.

Chapter 3: "Harnessing the Potential of AI-Powered Adaptive Learning in K12 Education"

Adaptive learning has been described as one of the most powerful tools in the modern education system, especially for use in K12 education. It is a type of computer-based educational technology that is designed to adjust instruction in order to meet the specific needs of the individual learner. Using artificial intelligence (AI), adaptive learning systems are capable of detecting a student's level of knowledge, and then delivering activities and content based on that knowledge. This innovation accelerates, extends, and deepens learning to individualize education.

One of the most powerful aspects of adaptive learning technology is its capacity to be dynamic. This means that the instruction and support received by a learner actively changes in response to their progress and performance, allowing a more tailored and successful experience. It is easily accessed from a variety of devices and easily implemented into existing teaching methods, making it one of the most efficient and cost-effective forms of educational technology.

There are numerous potential benefits of adaptive learning technology for K12 students. The most prominent advantage is the ability to individualize instruction, allowing teachers to deliver content to students based on their strengths, weaknesses, and current level of knowledge. This form of advanced customization levels the playing field for all students, providing them with an opportunity to enjoy a more effective, tailored, and personalized learning experience.

The data generated from an adaptive learning system is incredibly useful for teachers, providing them with an overview of the current performance of the students they serve. This allows educators to identify areas of improvement, as well as track the progress of their students over time. These insights can then be used to guide more effective instruction and provide proactive support to those who may be struggling.

Adaptive learning also has the potential to offer K12 students access to digital content beyond textbooks and other traditional teaching materials. Augmenting classroom instruction with the addition of video lessons and games, simulations and virtual labs or field trips, and integrating real-world data can all provide students with a more holistic learning experience. This can be especially beneficial for those who may benefit from visual or interactive learning material.

Innovative AI-driven adaptive learning technologies such as Intelligent Tutoring Systems (Its) have the potential to provide students with an entirely personalized learning experience. Such technologies facilitate an interactive experience by providing instant feedback and guidance as learners attempt to complete tasks or answer questions, ensuring that instruction is tailored to each individual student. This type of personalized support and guidance can enhance engagement and reinforce learning.

The implementation of AI-powered adaptive learning in K12 education holds an enormous amount of potential for both students and educators alike. Adaptive learning technology can facilitate a customized and personal learning experience for each student, offering tailored content, targeted support, and useful insights. Together, this allows for higher levels of engagement, deeper learning, and improved results. Therefore, it is clear that harnessing the potential of AI-powered adaptive learning technology in K12 education is a strategy well worth exploring.

Chapter 4: "Enabling Student Success Through AI-Powered Adaptive Learning".

In recent years, artificial intelligence (AI) has taken the education sector by storm, with increasing understanding of the potential of AI-powered adaptive learning for enabling student success. AI-powered adaptive learning applies algorithms and machine learning to provide a personalized education experience for each learner. This can involve providing personalized instruction and feedback, directing learners to content that suits their needs, and providing recommendations of other resources. In this way, adaptive learning systems have the potential to equip students with the skills, knowledge, and critical thinking abilities to achieve their educational goals.

The current pandemic has placed a greater emphasis on using digital technology for learning, creating challenges around access, quality, and equity. AI-powered adaptive learning can help to mitigate these challenges by providing data-driven recommendations to learners and educators that can bolster technology-driven instruction and learning. Adaptive learning can empower learners with personalized content, feedback, and subsequent instruction. With access to material tailored to each student's needs, targeted support can be provided and progress tracked in real-time.

AI-powered adaptive learning systems have the potential to enable student success through various interventions such as instructional scaffolding, tailoring instruction to individual learning styles and abilities, providing feedback in real-time, and using performance data to determine an individual's progress. Thus, data-driven adaptive learning systems can help educators more effectively target instruction and support strategies, supplementing traditional classroom instruction. Additionally, AI-powered systems can allow for automatic tracking of student progress, enabling teachers to quickly identify learning gaps in individual learners or in the class.

One of the major advantages of AI-powered adaptive learning when compared to traditional classroom instruction is the ability to scale. AI-powered adaptive systems are able to reach a larger number of students than what is possible with a single teacher. The scalability of adaptive learning systems also allows students to learn according to their own individual paces and preferences. Additionally, AI-powered systems can differentiate individual student profiles, enabling individualized recommendations and specific guidance for each learner. This helps to target instruction more effectively and promote self-directed learning, allowing students to gain deeper understanding of topics and construct knowledge for themselves.

AI-powered adaptive learning has the potential to enable student success by ensuring personalized instruction, feedback, and guidance are tailored to each learner and their needs. Adaptive learning helps to scale education and provide targeted content, while also providing students with the opportunity for self-directed learning. AI-powered adaptive learning can supplement traditional classroom instruction, helping to reach a larger range of learners and produce measurable results. It is an effective tool. today's educational landscape, and can help support teachers, learners, and parents in achieving educational goals.

Chapter 5: "Unlocking the Potential of AI-Powered Adaptive Learning for K12 Students"

Adaptive learning, sometimes referred to as 'personalized learning', is an innovative method of teaching and learning that uses data and artificial intelligence (AI) to provide students with an individualized and personalized learning experience.

In educational institutions, computer-aided instruction (CAI) and online learning have been used for decades to deliver educational content in an efficient and cost-effective way. These digital learning platforms continue to evolve and leverage advancements in technology to offer even more customized experiences to students. Increasingly, teachers are turning to AI-powered adaptive learning to further personalize instruction and better support the various learning needs and styles of individual students.

AI-powered adaptive learning is an instructional system that utilizes artificial intelligence to dynamically deliver personalized learning experiences to each student based on their previous performance, current level of understanding, and areas of strength. It works by leveraging data collected about each students' interests, abilities, and goals. This data is fed into an AI algorithm that constantly assesses and evaluates each student's mastery of complex material and develops individualized curricula that is tailored to their unique learning needs.

The potential of this advanced AI-driven technology is immense. In K-12 education, AI-powered adaptive learning can be used to create a personalized learning journey for each student, promote deeper engagement with the material, and accelerate the knowledge acquisition process. AI-based tools and techniques can also allow educators to better monitor and optimize the learning experience for each student, as well as more effectively identify and address areas of weakness.

By leveraging AI-powered adaptive learning solutions, K-12 educational institutions can enhance the efficiency and efficacy of their teaching and learning processes. The technology can help achieve better individual student results by providing tailored instruction based on individual learning styles, and by modifying and delivering content to match each student's progress and capabilities. The technology is also invaluable in identifying areas of strength and weakness. By using AI-driven technology, educators can gain valuable insights into each student's strengths and weaknesses and can adjust curricula accordingly.

AI-powered adaptive learning can create an engaging and interactive learning experience for K-12 students. Unlike traditional teaching methods, AI-powered solutions can be customized to match each student's real-life interests and develop curricula that are fun and engaging. Furthermore, AI-based technology can be used to monitor student engagement and gain insights into the motivation levels of each student.

AI-powered adaptive learning solutions offer great potential to enhance the effectiveness of instruction and engagement of students in K-12 educational institutions. By leveraging the power of AI to create individualized curricula, monitor engagement levels, and identify areas of weakness, teachers can ensure that students of all ability levels get the individualized attention and support they need to progress and grow. With AI-powered adaptive learning solutions, K-12 educational institutions can unlock its potential to improve learning outcomes and ensure that all students can unlock their full potential.

Chapter 6: "Leveraging AI-Powered Adaptive Learning to Transform K12 Education"

The idea of leveraging artificial intelligence (AI) and adaptive learning to transform K-12 education has become increasingly popular as educators and administrators strive to overcome traditional educational reforms. To put it simply, AI and adaptive learning allow for an individualized approach to instruction and curriculum, which can be tailored to the needs of every student, from early learners to high school seniors. AI-powered adaptive learning offers a far more efficient and effective way to educate K-12 students than traditional methods.

First, AI-powered adaptive learning algorithms are able to comprehend and evaluate every student's current learning state and identify the topics they struggle with or excel in. This capability is extremely beneficial for both in-person and online instruction, as it provides educators with a much greater understanding of each student's learning needs. Education teams are better equipped to make informed decisions about the best methods to use in order to help the student succeed.

Second, AI-powered adaptive learning algorithms are also able to dynamically adjust levels of difficulty to each student's needs. This is especially useful for online instruction, such as tutoring or personalized programs for students. AI-based technology can quickly adjust the level of difficulty to better suit the specific knowledge and ability of each student, allowing them to progress at their own pace.

Third, AI-powered adaptive learning algorithms are able to continuously adapt to the pupil's behavior and their learning progression. This is extremely beneficial as it helps in offering an improved, personalized approach for every individual student. Instead of having a set single lesson plan or programs for all the students,

AI-powered adaptive learning algorithms are able to ensure that the specific needs of each student are met, creating tasks that challenge their thinking in the best possible way.

Finally, AI-powered adaptive learning technology can be used to create digital learning insights which can be used by school faculty and administrators to better understand the learning needs of their students. AI-powered tools can offer actionable insights and key performance indicators (KPIs) that can inform educators to better allocate their resources and craft optimized curriculum.

AI-powered adaptive learning provides a revolutionary approach to the traditional methods of K-12 schooling. By creating a more personalized, efficient, and effective learning experience for students, AI-powered adaptive learning has the potential to revolutionize K-12 education. In leveraging the power of AI-powered adaptive learning tools to craft an individualized learning experience for each student, educators can empower their students to reach their greatest academic potential.

Chapter 7: "Unleashing the Power of AI-Powered Adaptive Learning in K12 Education"

AI-Powered Adaptive Learning has the potential to revolutionize the way k12 education is taught and experienced by both students and teachers. It's a method of learning where content is customized to an individual learner's needs and preferences. AI-Powered Adaptive Learning is especially powerful when applied to a k12 educational environment, because of its ability to quickly adjust to a student's pace of learning and the ability to standardize and store valuable learning data.

Adaptive learning takes advantage of AI-Powered algorithms, which is a type of software that can automate the process of learning a specific skill or knowledge. AI-Powered algorithms can be used to identify gaps in an individual student's learning and generate personalized learning paths, materials, and activities for them. These individualized learning paths are then tailored to each student's own individual strengths and weaknesses and can be adjusted over time as students gain more knowledge and understanding. This further benefits the teacher as they are able to personalize each student's learning in real-time.

Unleashing the power of AI-Powered Adaptive Learning in k12 education can help level the playing field for all students. This is especially true for students from disadvantaged backgrounds, where the access to resources and a higher quality of education may be limited. AI-Powered Adaptive Learning can help students in these scenarios gain access to a better quality education. AI-Powered Adaptive Learning can tailor each student's experience to their individual learning needs and preferences, making the learning process more engaging and enjoyable for everyone.

The ability to store and analyze a student's learning data can help both students and teachers significantly. Not only does it help teachers to create personalized learning paths for their students, but it also helps them to identify patterns in student behavior. This can in turn, help teachers to create effective ways in which to support students' learning and progress.

AI-Powered Adaptive Learning can help reduce educational costs. With traditional education models, educators and administrators need to invest in resources and materials designed for the entire group of students. With AI-Powered Adaptive Learning, educators and administrators can instead spend more time and money on the development of tailored educational resources which can be used by many students.

AI-Powered Adaptive Learning also helps to improve teacher productivity. With the use of AI-Powered algorithms, teachers can spend less time on administrative tasks such as setting up classes, lesson planning, and grading, as AI-Powered Adaptive Learning can reduce the complexity of such tasks. This allows teachers to spend more time focusing on the needs of their students and their development.

The power of AI-Powered Adaptive Learning in K12 education maximizes both the learning experience of students and the effectiveness of teachers. AI-Powered Adaptive Learning can be used to improve student engagement, performance, and academic success. This in turn, can lead to higher student retention rates and more motivated classrooms.

Chapter 8: "Unlock Student Potential With AI-Powered Adaptive Learning in K12 Education"

With the introduction of AI-powered adaptive learning (AL) into the K12 education system, students have immense potential to unlock their full learning potential. AL utilizes artificial intelligence (AI) to allow educational systems to quickly and easily customize the learning experience to better fit each student's individual needs and abilities. This approach to teaching and learning seeks to maximize the educational process and provide more personalized instruction that can seamlessly adjust as students' information and performance levels change.

There are numerous benefits associated with utilizing AL in the K12 educational system. One of the primary advantages is that it offers teachers and administrators the ability to monitor and gauge the progress of each student in order to better individualize their learning experiences. By being able to see how well a student is doing in various subjects and areas, teachers can adjust the strategies and activities they use with that specific student in order to give them the best chance at success. Additionally, AI-powered AL also provides teachers with extra time to focus on other classroom and administrative tasks.

For teachers, AL can be a valuable tool in helping them create a personalized and engaging learning environment. By utilizing AL, teachers can create individual lessons that target a student's individual strengths and weaknesses in order to better support them in their learning. Furthermore, AL allows for differentiated instruction which allows teachers to work with small groups and provide more tailored learning experiences for individual students. By providing personalized, tailored instruction, teachers can help foster a more meaningful learning process for each student.

For students, AL offers them a unique and engaging opportunity to unlock their full learning potential. By being able to customize their own learning experience, students can better focus on their content areas, adjust their lessons, and gain more autonomy in their educational process. Additionally, students also have the benefit of having their learning process constantly monitored by the AI system. This allows the AI to provide real-time feedback and insight into how well a student is doing thus providing them with timely support and the opportunity to identify any areas that they might need extra attention in.

Utilizing AI-powered adaptive learning (AL) in K12 education provides a unique opportunity for students to unlock their true potential. By providing personalized, engaging instruction that is tailored to each student's individual needs and abilities, AL offers an effective and highly efficient way for teachers to create meaningful learning environments. Furthermore, the use of AI-based technology allows teachers to keep track of student performance, provide real-time insight into students' progress, and offer immediate feedback when needed. Finally, students are able to better control and adjust their learning experiences in order to maximize their potential in the educational process. As AI-based technology continues to further refine AL, K12 education has the opportunity to provide an even more personalized and engaging learning experience for students.

Chapter 9: "Unleashing the Power of AI-Powered Adaptive Learning in K12 Education"

In the past few decades, the world of education has witnessed a massive technological transformation. Now, more than ever, artificial intelligence (AI) and adaptive learning has enabled teachers to provide personalized and tailored instruction to students at any level of academia. AI technology and adaptive learning are becoming popular among K12 educators who are looking for ways to give students a deeper and more meaningful education. K12 education needs to leverage the power of AI-driven adaptive learning in order to maximize student learning and development.

Adaptive learning is the process of an interactive, data-driven learning system that is personalized to the individual student. This system automatically adapts itself around the student's needs by providing a unique learning path suited to their background, interests, and learning preferences. AI algorithms assess the student's responses and continually inform the system of their knowledge, skills, and learning needs. Through this process, AI-powered systems help teachers provide tailored instruction and resources to help students learn at their own pace.

One major advantage of using AI-driven adaptive learning tools in K12 education is its ability to enable personalized instruction. AI-powered systems can identify the most effective learning paths tailored to an individual student's needs and interests. This helps to ensure that students are not retreading the same learning path every time and that their studying experiences are varied. With adaptive learning, individual students can benefit from targeted instruction, which helps them to make strides in their learning quickly.

Additionally, AI-driven adaptive learning platforms can help create a more engaging and enjoyable experience for students. In the past, students had to adhere to learning curriculums that were time-consuming and monotonous. Now, AI-powered systems allow for student-centric learning. In other words, students are able to break away from the traditional schooling frameworks and take their learning journey in a different direction. AI-driven adaptive learning empowers students to learn how to best learn through their own progress.

AI-driven adaptive learning can also be used to help predict student outcomes. By utilizing the data gathered by AI-powered systems, teachers are able to identify patterns in student behavior and to gain insights on the potential trajectories of individual student performance. With these insights, teachers can decide how best to focus their resources and support students in areas that are most likely to result in better outcomes.

In essence, AI-driven adaptive learning technology promises to revolutionize the way K12 students learn and develop. Through personalized instruction, a more engaging learning experience, and predictive analytics, teachers and administrators can maximize student potential and maximize the educational outcomes. The future of K12 education needs to leverage the power of AI-driven adaptive learning in order to help students reach their highest educational potential.

Chapter 10: "On the Cutting Edge: Exploring the Benefits of AI-Driven Adaptive Learning in K12 Education".

The modern education system is on the cutting edge of technology, and the use of artificial intelligence (AI)-driven adaptive learning in K12 education is one of the most important technological developments of the past decade. The application of AI has made it possible for educators to meet the ever-changing demands of a technology-savvy student population in a more efficient and effective way.

AI-driven adaptive learning involves the use of algorithms to detect a student's strengths and weaknesses, and then tailor the curriculum to those needs in real time. By leveraging the power of machine learning, AI-driven adaptive learning adjusts the instruction and content for each individual student to make sure that they are receiving the most beneficial instruction.

The advantages of AI-driven adaptive learning in K12 education extend far beyond simply helping students learn efficiently and effectively. This technology can actually help reduce dropout rates and improve academic achievement. By identifying a student's academic strengths and weaknesses, AI-driven adaptive learning can proactively intervene to prevent them from falling behind or abandoning their studies. Furthermore, by focusing on a student's individual needs, AI-driven adaptive learning can ensure that each student receives the most appropriate instruction to maximize their potential.

The application of AI in K12 education also provides educators with valuable insights into the way students learn. By using AI-driven adaptive learning, educators can gain a better understanding of where students struggle, where they excel, and what type of instruction is most beneficial for each particular student. Armed with this knowledge, educators can then determine which instructional strategies are most effective for different types of learners and implement them into the classroom.

In addition to providing educators with greater insights into how to better instruct different types of learners, AI-driven adaptive learning can also provide the opportunity to personalize instruction for each student. By tailoring the curriculum to the individual student's needs and preferences, students become more engaged and motivated to learn. This provides an opportunity for a more holistic education that is tailored to the individual.

AI-driven adaptive learning can help teachers save time in the classroom. By using AI-driven adaptive learning, teachers can automate certain tasks that would normally have to be done manually. This can free up more time for educators to focus on teaching, providing them with the opportunity to customize instruction to best fit the needs of their students.

AI-driven adaptive learning presents a wealth of opportunities to K12 educators. By leveraging the power of machine learning, AI-driven adaptive learning can enable educators to customize instruction to individual students, gain valuable insights into how students learn, and save time in the classroom. These benefits create an opportunity to create a more effective learning environment, helping students reach their full potential.

Chapter 11: "Harnessing the Power of AI for Personalized Learning in K12 Education"

Artificial Intelligence (AI) is becoming increasingly popular in the realm of educational technology. This technology offers the potential to revolutionize the ways students learn and educators teach. With AI, students can benefit from personalized learning experiences tailored to their individual academic needs. AI can also enable teachers to better manage their classrooms, quickly assess student performance, and personalize instruction in the classroom. AI can provide an unprecedented level of knowledge for educators to enhance the education of their students and help them reach their full potential.

One of the most important applications of AI to K12 education is its potential to create a personalized learning experience for each student. Personalized learning has the potential to revolutionize the way students approach learning. Rather than expecting all students to follow the same curriculum in the same way, AI will help identify the individual needs of each learner, and customized instruction can be designed to match those needs. AI can analyze data from various educational sources and recommend appropriate curricula and learning materials tailored to a specific student. Although this strategy requires initial input from educators, AI can become more adept over time in offering personalized learning pathways for students.

A further application of AI to K12 education is its potential to increase the efficiency and efficacy of classroom management. AI can analyze student data to identify patterns of behavior and generate insights into how a teacher can better manage their classroom. AI can also help educators monitor the progress of individual students and detect any developmental issues that need addressing. With advances in AI-based education technology, teachers can gain valuable insights into their students' learning patterns, which can help them modify their instruction accordingly and provide better-targeted support for their learners.

AI can also provide useful insights into student performance and enable teachers to quickly assess the success of their instruction. For example, AI could detect the logical patterns behind a student's work and be able to accurately gauge the student's understanding of the material. This kind of rapid feedback can help teachers focus on the topics students are having trouble with and help them revise the curriculum accordingly. Moreover, AI can provide real-time feedback for students, which can help them become aware of their mistakes and take corrective action quickly.

AI can also be leveraged to enable more personalization in instruction in the classroom. AI-based technologies can help teachers identify the strengths and weaknesses of their students and provide personalized solutions to improve student learning. AI can also help teachers generate custom course content that matches the individual needs of their students, thus allowing teachers to tailor their instruction and provide a more individualized learning experience.

AI is emerging as a powerful tool for K12 education. AI has the potential to revolutionize the ways educators teach their students and enable personalized learning that meets the individual academic needs of each student. AI can also help teachers increase the efficiency and efficacy of their instruction by providing valuable insights into student performance and helping them focus on topics that need more attention. Through these applications, AI can help K12 students reach their academic potential and realize their full potential.

Chapter 12: "Harnessing the Power of Adaptive AI to Maximize K12 Learning".

In today's world, artificial intelligence (AI) is quickly making a major impact on the way students learn within K12 classrooms. AI has the potential to revolutionize the educational process so that all students receive a more personalized, adaptive educational experience. With AI, teachers will be able to more easily track the progress of many students simultaneously, adapt content based on the educational needs of the student, and customize learning experiences to each student's abilities and interests.

AI can be used to create adaptive learning programs that respond to the student's immediate needs. These programs have the potential to provide personalized instruction based on the particular student's strengths, weaknesses, and interests. The potential power of AI is evident; it can generate content that is much more engaging and tailored to the individual student. This could eliminate the common issue of the "one size fits all" approach which results in some students becoming bored or unengaged. AI-driven adaptive systems can provide better content and more support which could mean improved grades and better learning outcomes for learners.

Regarding personalized instruction, AI can be used to create and monitor assessments and feedback loops. AI can be used to generate questions for tests which will provide each student with a more individualized, tailored assessment. AI-driven testing has the capacity to help identify areas of weakness in the student's understanding of a certain subject and quickly give them the appropriate kind of support and guidance. Additionally, AI can provide teachers with meaningful insights and feedback when it comes to assessing certain topics or areas of study.

Another area where AI can be leveraged for K12 educational purposes is in the implementation of educational simulations. Simulations have the capacity to demonstrate the consequences of a given action or decision, allowing the student to get an idea of what real-world scenarios actually look like and how different decisions can impact the outcome. Such simulations can help to build up a better understanding and higher level engagement with the material being presented by the teacher. AI-driven simulations can further be used to help improve student performance by providing feedback in the form of predictive analytics.

Using AI can help to optimize the teaching-learning cycle for each student. AI-driven systems are able to actively collect data, identify trends, and adjust lesson plans as a result. By being able to continuously fine-tune the material being taught, AI can help to keep the classroom atmosphere dynamic and engaging. AI-driven systems can also make grading more efficient and effective by providing help with grading tests, homework, and other assignments.

Harnessing the power of AI in K12 can lead to significant improvements for all students as all learners can benefit from a more personalized, adaptive learning experience. AI-driven systems have the potential to revolutionize K12 education by providing teachers and students with more meaningful insights and feedback, creating more engaging simulations, and optimizing the teaching-learning cycle for each student. In this way, AI can be used to maximize the potential of K12 learning.

Chapter 13: "Adapting to a Brighter Future: Exploring the Potential of AI-Powered Adaptive Learning in K12 Education"

Adapting to a brighter future and tapping into its potential is something that many people are striving to do in the field of K12 education. With rapid advances in Artificial Intelligence (AI) and advances in machine learning, adaptive learning is gaining significant momentum. AI-powered adaptive learning is aimed at providing personalized learning experiences for each student to meet their individual learning needs and improve their academic achievement.

Adaptive learning refers to an educational system in which the content and delivery are tailored to the individual student's level of understanding. In essence, AI-powered adaptive learning can be seen as an intelligent system of tutoring, when a computer learns to adapt to a student's characteristics, including their strengths and weaknesses. This system can be used to identify the student's current understanding and performance gaps. It can also suggest strategies to accommodate the student's unique learning style.

Among the many advantages of AI-powered adaptive learning in K12 education, its ability to be used as a highly effective supplemental teaching tool stands out. In comparison to traditional methods, it provides students with multiple methods of learning, which allows students to learn more effectively. AI-powered adaptive learning is designed to increase student interactivity and engagement, which can ultimately result in improved academic outcomes. As AI-powered adaptive learning systems are able to analyze the student's response to the content, they provide immediate feedback to the student. This allows the students to better understand the material and gain a deeper understanding.

By enabling personalized experiences for every student, AI-powered adaptive learning can also help close the achievement gap among different student groups. AI-powered systems are capable of inferring knowledge from data and tailoring the lesson according to the student's level of understanding. This eliminates the need for providing content that might not be appropriate for the student's level of knowledge. This also can bridge the gap between theoretical learning and application as AI-powered systems help students comprehend the material and apply it practically.

AI-powered adaptive learning systems can also help reduce the burden of teachers. AI-powered systems can reduce the need for teacher-directed classroom instruction and provide personalized learning experiences for every student. This can also save teachers time and allow them to focus on higher level tasks, such as providing guidance and feedback. AI-powered systems also provide comprehensive learning analytics, which can be used to assess the performance of students and customize the instruction.

For its academic benefits, AI-powered adaptive learning can also provide social and emotional benefits for students. AI-powered systems can teach students how to interact better with others as part of their educational journey. AI-powered systems can help to detect and respond to certain emotions in students, thus providing better support for them. Furthermore, AI-powered systems can detect and respond to behaviors and patterns, which can help students develop skills related to communication and collaboration.

AI-powered adaptive learning in K12 education has the potential to revolutionize the way students learn. It can provide personalized learning experiences for every student by adapting to each student's individual needs and abilities. AI-powered systems also provide insight into the performance of students and can help close the achievement gap among different student groups. Furthermore, AI-powered systems can reduce the burden of teachers and help to improve the social and emotional development of students. Ultimately, AI-powered adaptive learning can help students, teachers, and administrators alike, as they adapt to a brighter future.

Chapter 14: "Leveraging AI to Elevate K12 Student Outcomes: The Promise of Adaptive Learning"

The promise of leveraging Artificial Intelligence and adaptive learning in the K-12 education system is hugely exciting. By utilizing AI, educational institutions can more effectively personalize instruction for students of any age, enabling them to learn more effectively and quickly reach higher educational milestones. With this in mind, it is important to understand the potential of adaptive learning and its applications in K-12 education.

Adaptive learning is a form of educational technology that uses AI algorithms to tailor teaching methods to each student's individual strengths and weaknesses. It constantly adjusts and evolves based on student input and performance, providing personalized academic guidance and assistance designed for each individual student's needs. This type of tailored instruction can help minimize learning gaps while increasing instructional efficiency and the quality of education.

Adaptive learning helps foster an engaging learning environment by identifying and understanding each student's learning styles and educational needs and then making adjustments to the curriculum in response to that data. For instance, an AI-based algorithm can analyze student engagement over time, identifying topics or activities that appear to be of particular interest or difficulty for a student. It can then adjust the curriculum accordingly, tailoring activities and assessments around those areas to make sure the student is getting the best possible education. By doing this, adaptive learning can give each student a more comprehensive and engaged learning experience, leading to better educational outcomes.

Adaptive learning also utilizes data and analytics to allow teachers to better adapt to their students' needs. By making use of data-driven analysis, educators can more effectively monitor and measure each student's progress, quickly identify areas in which they may need help or further guidance, and tweak instructional methods to ensure that instruction is properly tailored to the student's specific needs. With regular and accurate feedback, teachers can track student performance over time and see which areas need improvement or acceleration.

Leveraging AI to elevate K-12 student outcomes also enhances interactive learning in the classroom. Using AI-infused tools such as virtual characters, avatar simulations, and interactive learning games, students can have more enjoyable learning experiences within the classroom. These approaches help deepen students' engagement by providing real-world connections and allowing students to actively explore different topics, thereby increasing their on the whole interest in the course material.

By leveraging AI and adaptive learning in K-12 education, it can bring about a unique learning environment that will ultimately lead to better educational outcomes for students of all ages. It can help create personalized learning experiences that are more engaging, more efficient, and more effective. By utilizing AI-driven models, data analytics, and interactive learning tools, interactive learning in the classroom can become more exciting and more meaningful, ultimately providing students with the best possible educational experience.

Chapter 15: "Unlocking the Potential of Adaptive Learning with AI Technology in K12 Education"

The potential of adaptive learning aided by Artificial Intelligence (AI) technology is being acknowledged by educational institutions around the world, in the K12 education set up in particular. Learning through adaptive learning is immensely beneficial to the student learning process, and integrating AI technology into the system can further leverage positive results.

Adaptive learning involves the acquisition of knowledge adapted to individual learners with educational software that is customized according to the learning needs and expectations of the individual student. Modern AI technology has the potential to further enhance this process, making the learning process an even more personalized and enjoyable experience. AI technology has been able to introduce personalized learning plans, assess the student's progress, and offer real-time feedback and personalized guidance.

AI technology can be used to analyze each student's academic performance and tailor instruction accordingly. The technology can also be used to develop the learner's ability to think critically and independently. By understanding the unique cognitive style of the student, programs can be designed to encourage learners to discover information and to take responsibility for their own learning.

AI technology can be used to help teachers customize instruction for individual students. Through an AI-supported platform, a teacher can assign appropriate tasks according to the student's interests, level of skill, and understanding. This technology can also enable teachers to create a learning plan for each individual student, thereby allowing them to give customized instruction to each student according to their needs.

AI technology can also act as an assistant to the teacher in managing the classroom environment. It can help teachers design an environment that is conducive to learning, by providing an accurate assessment of each student's current understanding and comprehension level. AI can also be used to customize the learning process for students, by tailoring instruction according to the student's learning style. This will lead to a more engaging and enjoyable learning experience.

AI has immense potential to improve the delivery of learning and instruction in the K12 education system. It can be used to speed up the process of acquiring knowledge, enabling students to learn more easily and efficiently. It can also help teachers to identify student weaknesses and provide them with appropriate interventions to assist them in overcoming challenges and improving their learning experience.

For helping students learn quickly and effectively, AI technology can also help create an inclusive learning atmosphere. It can allow teachers to promote diversity and inclusion in the classroom and increase student engagement. This will help create an environment where everyone is valued and respected.

AI technology in K12 education may seem intimidating, especially for teachers and administrators who are used to the traditional teaching methods. However, the potential benefits of integrating AI technology into a K12 educational system are immense and cannot be overlooked. With the proper implementation of AI technology, K12 education can be revolutionized, providing students with enriched and personalized learning experiences.

Chapter 16: "Leveraging AI-Powered Adaptive Learning to Empower K12 Students"

Artificial Intelligence (AI) has been making waves in the Education sector for a few years now, with advancements in Machine Learning, Natural Language Processing, and other related technologies being employed to improve, extend, facilitate, and enrich student learning experiences. AI-powered Adaptive Learning, i.e. the utilization of AI to personalize learning experiences for each student, has threaded itself as one of the core components of digital transformation in K12 education, thereby showcasing immense potential for improving student outcomes.

There are numerous benefits associated with AI-powered Adaptive Learning, and it can be employed as an effective tool for equipping K12 students with skills and knowledge that will help them become successful. By leveraging AI-powered Adaptive Learning, K12 students can be better prepared to meet the demands of higher education, as well as the increasingly competitive job market.

Initially, when AI was introduced to K12 education, its use was limited to basic automation and sophisticated analytics. But over the years, thanks to advancements in AI technology, its usage has extended to enable customized learning experiences. Adaptive Learning offers multiple advantages and opportunities for K12 students, such as personalized instruction, targeted assessments, and individualized enrichment resources, all of which can be tailored to meet their specific needs without sacrificing quality or teacher contact.

K12 students, especially those struggling with their academics, can benefit immensely from AI-powered Adaptive Learning by getting access to timely interventions and customized instruction that can help them catch up in their learning while simultaneously helping to bridge the achievement gap. AI-powered Adaptive Learning also provides opportunities for K12 students to explore and investigate on their own, allowing them to develop their critical thinking skills, as well as an understanding of the complexity of real-world problems.

Additionally, AI-powered Adaptive Learning can also increase student engagement, especially among those who may have previously been disinclined to learning. Tasks can be individualized with dynamic pedagogies that respond to individual student's capabilities, further adding to the on the whole learning experience. AI-powered Adaptive Learning can also be deployed to enable real-time decision-making, by helping teachers draw meaningful insights from student data to assess their level of understanding and offer immediate assistance as and when required.

AI-powered Adaptive Learning can also help teachers streamline their workflow, by making it easier to replicate courses,, set-up assignments, automate grading and give feedback, and manage administrative activities. This, in turn, will enable them to focus more on their primary job of providing quality instruction and guidance to students which can result in better student outcomes.

With all the potential AI-powered Adaptive Learning has to offer, K12 students stand to benefit most from it. It can enable them to acquire the skills and knowledge necessary to make them successful and competitive in the increasingly complex job market, while making learning more enjoyable and productive at the same time. AI-powered Adaptive Learning can be a powerful tool for K12 students to truly learn, and for educators to truly teach.

Chapter 17: "Unleashing the Potential of AI-Powered Adaptive Learning in K12 Education"

The explosion of technology in the 21st century has been nothing short of revolutionary. With the advent of artificial intelligence (AI), the education sector has seen a massive uptick in access to new and powerful educational tools, most notably adapting the concept of "adaptive learning" into the K12 space. Adaptive learning is founded on the basis that each learner is unique, with different goals, needs, levels, and interests. Fostering an understanding of these differences and providing tailored learning solutions to meet them is a key factor in fostering educational success for each student.

At its most basic level, AI-powered adaptive learning is a technology-based process of analyzing student responses to questions, information, and tasks before providing the learner with relevant and unique content and feedback that best suit their individual needs. By collecting and tracking data in order to personalize the classroom experience, K12 educators are able to make better-informed decisions and optimize learning outcomes for all learners in the classroom.

Innovative organizations like Google Classroom and Edmund are paving the way for adaptive learning techniques to enter the K12 space. With the help of these platforms, teachers are able to break down core academic content into smaller chunks of information or tasks to better personalize the learning experience. This method allows each student to develop a mastery of the material in their own unique way, without feeling overwhelmed or stuck.

Other applications of AI-powered adaptive learning are becoming increasingly ubiquitous in K12 classrooms. For example, data-driven chatbots are now being utilized to supplement and extend learning sessions through meaningful two-way conversations with students.

Furthermore, robots are being used in some school districts to provide feedback to learners that is specifically tailored to their level of understanding. By using data-driven algorithms to analyze student progress, feedback sheets can be tailored to each student's individual needs.

Another important application of AI-powered adaptive learning is its ability to provide enhanced timeline-focused learning. By tracking the progression of the learner through a particular curriculum, AI technology can facilitate the substitution of advanced or supplemental topics if the learner has progressed faster than expected. Furthermore, AI-powered adaptive learning can be used to provide additional practice and motivation on material that the learner has not yet fully grasped, thus ensuring that understanding of topics is maintained across different grade levels.

The potential of AI-powered adaptive learning in K12 education is immense. By giving students the opportunity to learn at their own pace, customized content, and feedback tailored specifically to their individual needs, educators are better equipped to provide the appropriate support to foster student success. Moreover, by collecting data from and providing interventions to each learner, K12 schools are able to ensure that all students reach a high level of understanding and mastery of the given content. In short, harnessing the power of AI-powered adaptive learning is a game-changer for K12 teachers and students alike.

Chapter 18: "Unlocking the Potential of AI-Powered Adaptive Learning in K12 Education"

As technology progresses exponentially, and our world becomes more reliant on Artificial Intelligence (AI) powered systems, it is important to consider how AI-powered adaptive learning can be utilized within the K12 educational system. AI-powered adaptive learning is the process of using machine learning algorithms to customize content for students based on their skills, abilities, and comprehension. Through this approach to education, teachers have the potential to accurately gauge student's progress, making instruction more effective.

Adaptive learning methods are achieved using a combination of AI techniques such as natural language processing, machine learning, and deep learning. The AI algorithms are able to assess the individual student's progress and recommend the next best step for them to take. This is in stark contrast to traditional educational methods, where the teacher teaches the same content to all students—regardless of their individual skills and abilities.

One of the major benefits of AI-powered adaptive learning is its ability to provide personalized content for each student. Rather than having a one-size-fits-all approach to instruction, the AI-powered system can tailor the approach and content to fit each individual student. In doing so, it can better address the learning gaps or areas of need of each student and strengthen the whole mastery of the subject. Additionally, adaptive learning can help reduce the need for rote memorization of facts, enabling each student to use the information to construct meaningful knowledge.

Besides, the user interface leveraged by AI-powered adaptive learning solutions enables students to remain engaged throughout the learning process. Responding in real-time to changes in the student's skills, abilities, and comprehension, the AI-driven system can adjust and adapt the content to fit the needs of the student. With an engaging, sensor-driven platform, students will remain interested and motivated to learn.

Furthermore, with AI-powered adaptive learning, teachers have access to greater data and insights into each student's educational progress. From measuring course navigation speed to the sequences of questions answered correctly, teachers can gain valuable insight into the learning process and adapt their instruction accordingly. As a result, teachers can improve the quality of instruction by fine-tuning approaches and adapting the subject to the student.

AI-powered adaptive learning enables K12 educators to assess their students in a consistent, standardized way. By leveraging Big Data and analytics, the AI algorithm can detect patterns in the data and set individualized goals for each student. By having consistent, data-driven assessments, teachers can accurately track the progress of their students to ensure they are meeting the educational objectives.

AI-powered adaptive learning solutions are a powerful tool for K12 education. Through adaptive learning, teachers can take a more personalized approach to instruction, enabling them to provide tailored content to fit the student's individual skills and abilities. Additionally, adaptive learning platforms have engaging user interfaces that motivate students to remain involved in the learning process. With access to personalized data and analytics, teachers can more accurately track each student's educational progress. Finally, adaptive learning systems enable teachers to assess students in a consistent, standardized way. AI-powered adaptive learning has the potential to revolutionize K12 education, unlocking new levels of student success, engagement, and mastery of the material.

Chapter 19: "Unlocking the Potential of AI-Powered Adaptive Learning in K12 Education"

As technology becomes more efficient and accessible, the potential applications of Artificial Intelligence (AI) in K12 education have grown considerably. One of the most promising areas is the field of AI-powered adaptive learning, which is quickly becoming an important tool for teachers looking to provide students with personalized educational experiences. Adaptive learning systems use AI to collect, analyze, and interpret data to provide students with tailored learning experiences. By offering personalized learning experiences, these systems can help to engage students more effectively, leading to higher levels of academic achievement.

AI-powered adaptive learning systems are designed to adapt to a student's individual needs and learning style. Since every student is different, these systems provide tailored resources to help them acquire knowledge faster. Adaptive systems can analyze student data such as reading level, test scores, and other metrics in order to better understand their capabilities and interests. Based on this data, the system can provide students with specialized resources to help them progress through their studies. This could include personalized activities, lessons, and assessments. AI-powered adaptive systems are also able to track a student's performance over time, allowing teachers to better customize their instruction.

One of the main advantages of using AI-powered adaptive learning is that it can reduce the amount of time teachers spend on administrative tasks. Since the system can provide students with personalized content and track individual progress, they can free up time to focus on instructional strategies. AI-powered adaptive systems can also help to identify areas of improvement and provide feedback, allowing teachers to customize their instruction accordingly.

AI-powered adaptive learning has numerous potential applications in K12 education. It can be used to support problem-solving, encourage critical thinking, and increase engagement in classes. AI-powered adaptive learning systems can also help to identify topics or concepts that students may have difficulty understanding and provide appropriate resources to address those issues.

AI-powered adaptive learning can also be used to promote collaboration and engagement among students. By providing personalized experiences, AI-powered adaptive systems can help to foster a sense of community in the classroom. The system can be used to track how students interact with each other and provide resources to help them build strong relationships.

One of the challenges associated with AI-powered adaptive learning is that it requires access to technology and adequate resources in order to be properly implemented. For those in underprivileged regions or areas, access to adaptive learning resources is often limited. To overcome this challenge, some districts have begun using training programs and partnerships to educate educators on how to utilize AI-powered adaptive learning systems.

AI-powered adaptive learning has the potential to revolutionize the K12 educational system. By providing tailored resources, it can help to engage students and provide them with personalized educational experiences. As access to these resources becomes more available, we can expect to see more AI-powered adaptive learning systems being used in classrooms around the world.

Chapter 20: "Unlocking the Potential of AI-Powered Adaptive Learning in K12 Education"

In recent years, Artificial Intelligence (AI) has gained an increasingly important role in the education sector. AI-powered adaptive learning can help K-12 education unlock the potential of individual students by providing personalized education to each student. It can also improve the on the whole teaching and learning process by providing timely feedback, data-driven insights, and guidance on best practices for teacher and student engagement.

Adaptive learning is the process of delivering personalized instruction and support to individual learners through the use of data-driven algorithms that continually adjust the pace, order, and complexity of learning content based on a student's progress. Adaptive learning is unique from other types of instruction because it focuses on individual student needs rather than on the entire class. By customizing instruction, educators are able to ensure that learners are receiving content and support that is relevant to their current knowledge level in a timely manner. In addition, AI-powered adaptive learning systems collect data that allow teachers to gain insights into student performance and make data-driven decisions about instructional materials and strategies.

AI-powered adaptive learning has many potential benefits for K-12 educators. For instance, AI-powered systems can identify and respond to individual learning needs quickly, allowing educators to individualize instruction. This can be especially helpful in providing content to non-traditional learners, such as those who are English language learners (Ells) or students with special needs. Adaptive learning platforms also help teachers quickly identify gaps in student knowledge, which can then be addressed in real-time, allowing them to take corrective action early in the learning process.

In addition to providing data-driven individualized instruction and feedback, AI-powered adaptive learning platforms offer K-12 educators tools to reduce the amount of time needed for grading or providing feedback. AI-powered systems are able to quickly analyze wide amounts of data and provide detailed feedback to teachers on individual and group student performance, making it possible for educators to spend less time grading and more time interacting with students. AI-powered systems are also able to detect patterns in student responses in order to quickly identify misconceptions and ensure accuracy.

AI-powered adaptive learning systems also provide K-12 educators with data-driven insights into student engagement and performance. AI-powered systems can track student progress and provide timely feedback to teachers on areas of improvement. This data can also be used to inform instruction, as teachers can make data-driven adjustments to ensure each student is being challenged and properly supported in their learning.

AI-powered adaptive learning can have a positive impact on K-12 learning by providing personalized instruction, reducing teacher workload, and enabling data-driven decisions. AI-powered systems can help K-12 educators gain insight into student performance and engagement, allowing them to make data-driven decisions that help ensure students are receiving the best possible education. By unlocking the potential of AI-powered adaptive learning, K-12 educators can ensure that all students have access to the individualized instruction they need to succeed.

Chapter 21: "Leveraging AI-Powered Adaptive Learning for Successful K12 Education Outcomes"

When it comes to promoting educational success, many school districts are turning to technology-rich solutions such as leveraging AI-powered adaptive learning. Adaptive learning is based on the belief that students learn best when instruction, curriculum, and assessment are tailored to the individual.

AI-powered adaptive learning is a technology-based approach to instruction that responds in real-time to the individual needs and abilities of students. Through the integration of data and intelligent algorithms, AI-powered adaptive learning tools tailor instruction, deliver timely feedback, and continually assess student progress. For K-12 education, these tools are particularly beneficial as they can be used to deliver personalized instruction, promote self-regulation and learning, and enhance on the whole student engagement.

AI-powered adaptive learning is particularly crucial in achieving successful K-12 education outcomes. By utilizing such tools, teachers and school districts can more easily identify learning gaps and tailor instruction accordingly. AI-powered adaptive learning uses data-driven learning pathways and engages students at their own pace while still teaching towards the intended learning goal. AI-powered adaptive learning can also provide tailored assessment for each student, aiding in the development of better individual learning plans. As a result, students can receive instruction and evaluation at an appropriate level for their ability, leading to a greater likelihood of successful education outcomes.

AI-powered adaptive learning also aids in the early identification of learning challenges and helps to ensure that students have access to more timely interventions and improved learning strategies. AI-powered adaptive learning can make the collection, analysis and visualization of data faster and easier, which gives teachers access to deeper insights into student abilities and learning strategies. This data can be used to identify patterns, intervene in a more timely fashion, and adjust instruction and expectations accordingly. This deeper understanding of the individual student promotes a more targeted approach to learning and assessment and can help school districts measure student progress, competence, and achievement more accurately.

AI-powered adaptive learning offers many advantages and potential solutions to the challenge of improving K-12 education outcomes. Through the implementation of AI-powered adaptive learning, school districts can promote personalized instruction, timely feedback, and continual assessment of student progress. AI-powered adaptive learning can also help school districts identify learning gaps, provide appropriate learning strategies, and adjust instruction and expectations to better reflect the individual student. Through the use of AI-powered adaptive learning, school districts can ensure students have the tools they need to be successful in their educational endeavors.

Chapter 22: "Leveraging AI to Enhance K12 Learning: Unleashing the Power of Adaptive Education"

In the modern world of education, technology has revolutionized and transformed learning and teaching processes. One of the new and promising technologies that continues to be developed is AI, or artificial intelligence. AI has the potential to revolutionize the way knowledge is acquired, interpreted, and applied. By leveraging AI to enhance K12 learning, educators can create an adaptable and adaptive learning environment that eliminates rigid adherence to traditional pedagogy, and orients students to more sophisticated, AI based learning.

The potential of AI to transform K12 learning is great and evident. AI can enable better student engagement by promoting personalized and context-driven teaching and learning. AI can provide real-time analysis of students' progress and provide automated feedback and instruction to complement human intervention. AI can be used to optimize the way school systems are managed by designing efficient feasibility studies, for example, regarding student placement and attendance, teaching and administrative staff management, implementing a digital curriculum, and enacting a data-driven approach to teaching and learning. By leveraging AI to enhance K12 learning, educators can focus on more crucial tasks such as providing students with a better education.

Empowered by AI, K12 learning systems can be accelerated by providing personalized instruction, exposing students to concepts they might not otherwise have the opportunity to learn, and providing continual feedback and assessments. AI can provide instant answers, adjust the learning pace for individual students through automated tracking and feedback, and engage students through interactive and real-life activities. AI can also enable classroom games, virtual reality simulations, video games, and other creative tools for teaching, in order to engage students more effectively and foster more active learning.

Smart AI-based assessment systems can also be leveraged to provide personalized scores which can be used to determine the learning needs of students, track their progress over time, and inform teaching models. AI can also serve as an invaluable tool for empirically studying student performance, and identify key areas of improvement.

Most importantly, AI can play a key role in providing teachers the necessary insights in order to obtain an on the whole view of a school's performance, such as on-track attendance and graduation rates. By utilizing AI-based technology for data-driven decision-making, school administrators can gain access to educational trends, gaps within the system, and students' progress. This insight can be used to make effective and replicable changes such as providing resources where most needed, identifying key areas for improvement, and providing targeted support to teachers.

AI systems have the potential to revolutionize the way we teach and learn, and its effects can be particularly profound in K12 learning. By leveraging AI in K12 learning systems, educators can create an effective and adaptable learning environment that equips them with the necessary tools to provide personalized instruction and continual feedback. Such a system allows for a greater emphasis on learning objectives, improved results, and the capacity to track progress over time. AI can also allow school administrators to identify potential areas of improvement, and provide support and resources where most needed. Ultimately, leveraging AI for enhancing K12 learning can elevate learning outcomes and unearth the potential of technology for transforming the educational experience.

Chapter 23: "Harnessing the Power of AI and Adaptive Learning for K12 Education"

In the modern classrooms of today, AI and adaptive-learning solutions are revolutionizing the way instruction is delivered in K12 education. Artificial Intelligence (AI) and Adaptive-Learning offer new opportunities to innovate in education, allowing teachers to personalize the learning experience for each student. AI and adaptive-learning technologies offer unprecedented levels of analysis, exciting new learning opportunities, and transformative experiences that are helping to level the academic playing field.

The most fundamental way AI and adaptive-learning are impacting K12 education is by improving the ability to deliver personalized learning experiences. AI and adaptive-learning technologies make it possible to identify individual learning deficiencies or areas of strengths quickly with data that is generated in real-time. Teachers can then use this knowledge to create customized, tailored lesson plans that cater to the individual student's needs. With AI-driven adaptive learning, each student can progress at their own pace, meaning they never fall behind or suffer from the boredom of waiting on the rest of the class.

AI and adaptive-learning are also providing teachers and administration with an unprecedented level of insight into the learning process. AI-driven analytics can be used to track a student's progress in real-time, allowing teams to quickly identify any areas where students may be struggling and adjust the plan of instruction accordingly. AI can also be used to detect any cognitive patterns the student may exhibit, giving educators valuable knowledge as to how to best engage the student.

AI and adaptive-learning technologies are helping teachers to quickly access valuable teaching material that is both pertinent and engaging for their students. AI-driven search engines can easily sift through vast libraries of knowledge, creating customized, filtered content that is tailor-made for the learning objectives of the class. This saves instructors an enormous amount of time, as it eliminates the work of scrolling through irrelevant material when locating teaching resources.

AI and adaptive-learning technologies are helping to level the academic playing field by providing students with access to supplemental educational materials. Indeed, AI-driven online tutoring provides students with higher levels of support and guidance from outside the classroom, allowing them to fill in educational gaps and gain knowledge that they may have otherwise not had access to.

AI and adaptive-learning solutions are revolutionizing K12 education, allowing teachers to deliver personalized instruction, gain unprecedented insight into the learning process, access pertinent teaching material quickly, and help to level the academic playing field. As AI-driven technologies continue to develop and evolve, the opportunities for experimentation and innovation in K12 education are growing exponentially.

Chapter 24: "Harnessing the Power of Adaptive Learning for K12 Students".

Adaptive learning is a powerful tool in K12 education. It has the potential to support students' academic growth and development and improve their academic performance. Adaptive learning leverages technology and personalized instruction to empower students to take an active role in their learning. This method of learning shifts the focus from the teacher to the student, allowing for real-time feedback and support that can be tailored to the individual student's needs.

Adaptive learning is based on the idea that every student learns differently. It is designed to identify and address areas in which a student may be struggling. By typically incorporating assessments, adaptive learning platforms can adapt instruction to the student's level of understanding, allowing instruction to be delivered in a way that is more effective for the individual learner.

Adaptive learning can provide a variety of benefits to K12 students. First, adaptive learning can help students stay on track with their lesson plans. By providing targeted instruction, adaptive learning can help prevent students from falling behind in their studies and reduce the chances of them being overwhelmed by the content they are learning. The personalized instruction also promotes engagement and motivation among students, as it encourages them to take ownership of their own learning. Additionally, because adaptive learning is highly-individualized, it can present subjects in a more personalized, digestible manner, breaking down large topics into smaller, more manageable chunks.

Adaptive learning also can help improve student achievement. Research studies have found that students who used adaptive learning software performed better academically than students who did not. Furthermore, with the help of adaptive learning, instructors can easily keep track of a student's progress and provide additional support where needed. This type of one-on-one attention can be beneficial to students who may not be responding as well as they should to traditional instructional methods.

While adaptive learning has the potential to be a highly valuable tool in K12 education, there are some factors to consider. Firstly, implementing adaptive learning platforms can be costly, as it requires the need to invest in the necessary technology and tools. This can be an issue for schools that do not have the necessary resources. Additionally, there is the issue of privacy, as adaptive learning can collect vast amounts of data from its users. It is important that schools exercise caution when collecting this data, ensuring that it is properly safeguarded and securely stored.

Ultimately, the implementation of adaptive learning in K12 settings is a decision that must be carefully considered. While it has the potential to provide a more effective and engaging learning experience for students, schools must ensure that the necessary resources and safeguards are in place.

Chapter 25: "Harnessing the Power of AI to Unlock Adaptive Learning in K12 Education"

The use of Artificial Intelligence (AI) in education is rapidly increasing as a way to unlock the potential of personalized adaptive learning for K12 students. AI in education can be used in a variety of ways, such as providing feedback to teachers, analyzing student data to identify areas of difficulty, and delivering personalized content to each student. While AI promises to revolutionize K12 education, it also presents challenges that must be addressed in order for it to effectively improve learning outcomes. This paper will explore the benefits and challenges associated with harnessing the power of AI in K12 education, as well as potential solutions for overcoming them.

To begin, let's start by examining some potential benefits of using AI in K12 education. First, AI is starting to make the process of teaching and learning more efficient and effective. For example, AI can be used to deliver personalized content to each student based on their previous learning behavior and performance. This can reduce teacher workloads and enable teachers to focus their energy on topics which best suit the needs of each student. AI can also be used to automate grading and assessment processes, eliminating the need for tedious manual assessments and giving teachers more time to focus on teaching rather than grading.

In addition, AI can be used to better support differentiated learning for students of all ability levels. For example, AI can be used to continuously analyze student data and performance and provide feedback so that the educator can adjust their teaching style to best fit the needs of the student. AI can also improve access to educational content for all students, by providing personalized recommendations tailored to different interests and learning styles. Finally, AI can be used to create personal learning pathways that can adapt and evolve as the student's needs change.

As promising as AI in K12 education can be, there are also challenges that must be addressed before utilizing it to its fullest potential. First, AI requires a lot of data in order to be effective. Schools and districts must ensure they have the data they need in order to use AI effectively. AI is also only as valuable as the decisions that educators make in determining how to use it. Educators must be careful to use AI in such a way that it actually benefits student learning, rather than relying on it too heavily and allowing it to become a substitute for human instruction.

Furthermore, AI is not a one size fits all solution and still requires human judgment and decision-making in order to be effective. AI systems can make mistakes, and they can be biased and prone to errors. Educators must ensure that they are using AI ethically and within the bounds of educational and legal standards. Finally, AI can be expensive and schools and districts must weigh the cost of implementing AI systems against the potential benefits of using them.

In order to maximize the potential of AI in K12 education, schools and districts must acknowledge the challenges associated with it and develop strategies for addressing them. Educators should ensure that they have enough data to effectively use AI before attempting to do so. Additionally, educators must be sure to use AI in an ethical manner and consult with experts in the fields of AI and education when most effectively leveraging it. Finally, educators should focus on the beneficial outcomes of using AI, and strive to ensure that AI is used to enhance, rather than replace human instruction.

By taking these steps, schools and districts can lead the way in harnessing the power of AI to unlock adaptive learning for K12 students. By capitalizing on the potential of AI, schools and districts can ensure that students are best equipped to succeed in an ever-changing world.

Chapter 26: "A New Path to Success: The Benefits of AI-Powered Adaptive Learning in K12 Education"

Adaptive learning is an innovative educational technology that uses artificial intelligence (AI) and other advanced methods to deliver a tailored learning experience to students, based on their abilities and preferences. This type of personalized learning has the potential to revolutionize education in the K-12 sector, bringing countless benefits to both educators and learners.

Adaptive learning offers numerous advantages, such as time-saving and cost-effectiveness. AI-driven technologies can automate tedious tasks such as grading and assessment, removing the burden faced by educators in the testing and assessment of student's progress. Automation also allows educators to move away from traditional, manual-based assessment and focus more on personalized instruction, providing learners with a more enjoyable learning experience. AI-driven technologies also provide a wealth of data and analytics on a student's performance, which can be used to develop an individualized learning path that is tailored to the student's unique needs.

Adaptive learning also has the potential to increase learning outcomes and academic performance. AI-driven methods of education have been shown to have positive impacts on student engagement, helping learners remain interested and motivated in their course material. By offering individualized, personalized instruction, AI-enabled adaptive learning systems are also able to provide much more customized learning plans for individual students, helping them to grasp concepts more easily and progress faster.

The educational system also stands to gain from the implementation of adaptive learning in the K-12 sector. AI-driven technology can help bridge the ever-widening gap between students of different socio-economic backgrounds by providing learners from even the least advantaged backgrounds with the same level of education. This also has the potential to open up new educational opportunities to students who might otherwise not have access to them.

Adaptive learning can also help reduce the attainment gap between different schools, and contribute to quality assurance. By providing constant assessment of learning progress, AI-driven technology can provide educators with a better understanding of student performance and make sure that all students are given the tools they need to succeed.

AI-enabled adaptive learning has the potential to revolutionize education in the K-12 sector, and contribute to improved academic performance and attainment outcomes. The time saving and cost-savings offered by automated tasks, coupled with the potential for personalized, individualized instruction make adaptive learning a worthwhile investment. The technology can help bridge educational gaps between different schools and socio-economic backgrounds, and open up possibilities for learners who may not have had access to educational opportunities due to their background. With AI-driven adaptive learning, educators have a clear path to success that can bring countless benefits to both them and their students.

Chapter 27: "Unleashing the Power of AI-Enabled Adaptive Learning for K12 Students"

The power of AI-enabled adaptive learning can create wonderful learning opportunities for K12 students in the classroom and beyond. AI-enabled adaptive learning is a form of teaching and learning that uses technology, such as Artificial Intelligence (AI), to personalize instruction so that it adjusts to the individual learning needs of students. The technology works by taking into account factors such as competency, experience and content preferences when delivering instruction. This helps students discover and build on their skills and interests at a rate tailored to their particular abilities and needs.

The need for AI-enabled adaptive learning in K12 education is becoming more pressing than ever before. This is due to the ever-growing demands placed upon the education system to meet the needs of an increasingly diverse student population. To meet this challenge, many schools are turning to AI-enabled adaptive learning as a way of providing tailored instruction to meet the needs of their students.

One of the greatest advantages of AI-enabled adaptive learning is that it can deliver personalized, targeted instruction that is tailored to the individual needs of each student. This can help students develop the skills they need in order to achieve success in the classroom. AI-enabled adaptive learning can also increase engagement levels among students, motivate them to take initiative, and foster a greater appreciation for learning. It can also enable students to work independently and at their own pace with minimal direction or supervision.

The use of AI-enabled adaptive learning can also benefit teachers in a variety of ways. By providing tailored instruction to each student, the teacher can create a learning environment that is more engaging. They can also save time by using the AI-enabled system to efficiently deliver targeted instruction to each student. This can in turn lead to much more efficient classroom management, freeing up more time for the teacher to focus on building relationships with their students and providing personalized mentoring.

In addition to the personalized instruction that AI-enabled adaptive learning can provide, it can also increase student achievement. For example, AI-enabled adaptive learning can help identify knowledge gaps in students and subsequently guide them towards content that will help them fill in those gaps and understand the subject better. Additionally, since the system is constantly adapting to the needs of the student, it can help to ensure that their instruction is always up-to-date and relevant to their education.

The power of AI-enabled adaptive learning can be unleashed in K12 education in many ways. First, schools should look into the development of "adaptive classrooms". AI-enabled technology should be integrated into the learning environment to provide customized instruction. This can be used to supplement traditional teaching techniques and provide more tailored instruction to students. AI-supported learning systems can also be used to give teachers real-time feedback and advice.

Secondly, AI-enabled adaptive learning should be incorporated into learning management systems. Integrated adaptive learning systems can track students' learning progression and provide individualized instruction to each student based on their individual learning needs. Additionally, educational institutions should look into the development of AI-based assessment tools that can accurately assess each student's understanding of the material. This can provide the teacher with valuable data and insights in how to better target their instruction for their individual students.

AI-enabled adaptive learning should be utilized in teacher professional development. Professional development tools powered by AI can track the progress of teachers and help them identify areas where they could use improvement or assistance. Moreover, intelligent assessment systems can be used to track educator effectiveness and give valuable feedback for teachers to use when crafting lesson plans and improving their instructional skills.

The potential to unlock the power of AI-enabled adaptive learning for K12 students is limitless. There is a great opportunity to utilize this powerful technology to personalize instruction and create an environment of learning that is tailored specifically to individuals' needs and abilities. This could be a major step forward in improving the quality of education for students in K12 education today.

Chapter 28: "Unleashing the Power of AI-Enabled Adaptive Learning in K12 Education"

AI-Enabled Adaptive Learning is an emerging concept in K12 education that offers tremendous potential for revolutionizing how students learn. Adaptive learning combines artificial intelligence and machine learning techniques to create unique learning experiences for each student. By leveraging the power of AI-enabled algorithms, adaptive learning provides students with personalized lessons that adapt to their individual learning styles, ensuring that each student is able to acquire the necessary knowledge at their own pace.

At the core of AI-enabled adaptive learning is data. By monitoring the behavior of individual students during each lesson, the system records information such as how long it takes to complete a task, which areas are most difficult for the student, and which activities the student enjoys most. This data is then analyzed to produce a personalized curriculum tailored to the student's needs.

The advantage of AI-enabled adaptive learning is that it can be deployed at scale. Instead of having to create a unique curriculum for each student, an adaptive learning system can quickly adapt the teaching material to the needs of the student. This creates an agile and responsive learning environment that is capable of meeting the ever-changing requirements of the modern K12 classroom. Additionally, AI-enabled adaptive learning has been seen to drastically shorten the time needed for a student to master a subject or skill-set.

One of the main benefits of AI-enabled adaptive learning is improved engagement. By creating personalized lessons, students are able to maintain their focus and quickly acquire mastery. Furthermore, with the data collected by the system, teachers are able to tailor the material to each student, giving them the individual attention they may require. As such, AI-enabled adaptive learning can be a powerful tool for addressing learning disparities between students.

AI-enabled adaptive learning also offers several potential benefits for school administrators. As the system constantly adjusts to the student's needs, it can help streamline the teaching process, reducing the workload of teachers and allowing them to focus on providing instruction. It can also detect weak points in the curriculum, giving administrators an opportunity to make the necessary changes in order to provide the best possible educational experience for their students.

AI-enabled adaptive learning provides K12 education with an unprecedented level of flexibility and responsiveness that can revolutionize the way teachers and students interact. By leveraging the power of data and machine learning techniques, adaptive learning enables a personalized and engaging learning experience for each student. It also allows teachers and administrators to be better prepared for the ever-changing needs of K12 students and the modern-day K12 classroom.

Chapter 29: "Harnessing the Potential of AI for Enhanced K12 Educational Experiences"

In the modern world, artificial intelligence (AI) is increasingly being used to revolutionize the way classrooms are managed, increase classroom productivity and ultimately, enhance the educational experience of K-12 students. AI-based technologies have already enabled greater collaboration and communication among students, while enabling teachers to focus their attention on individual students' needs. At the same time, these technologies are providing personalized learning environments for students of all ages and academic levels, helping to improve their ability to comprehend, retain and effectively apply what they learn within the classroom setting.

By leveraging AI, teachers can access vast amounts of data in order to tailor content to a student's level of understanding and ability. AI-based tools provide teachers with detailed data on each student's academic performance, learning objectives, academic achievement and behavior; and by harnessing this data, teachers can customize instruction to fit the needs of each student individually. Additionally, with tools like voice-activated virtual assistants, teachers can quickly and easily access additional educational resources for their classroom, or even assist in the remote monitoring of student activity.

Another key benefit of AI lies in its ability to generate personalized learning plans for students. By using AI-based algorithms, teachers can easily combine historical data, assessment scores, and other information to develop an individualized plan for each student. In addition, AI can be used to generate data which helps teachers identify areas of potential development and improvement and plan accordingly, or check for any potential gaps in the students' learning and skill.

AI and machine learning tools are being employed to help students increase their engagement, participation, and performance within the classroom. These systems do so by enabling teachers to assess individual students' progress and performance more accurately and quickly. They can also be employed in tracking the on the whole performance of the entire classroom, allowing for faster and more accurate performance assessment and inter-student comparison.

The potential of AI to improve the K-12 education experience is vast and impressive. The data driven insights that AI provides can be used to better tailor instruction, optimize learning plans, track student performance and engagement, and more. AI-based solutions are already being used in K-12 classrooms around the world, helping to make the educational experience increasingly meaningful, efficient, and successful. Ultimately, AI holds the key to revolutionizing our classrooms and enhancing the learning experiences of today's students.

Chapter 30: "Unleashing the Potential of AI-Powered Adaptive Learning in K12 Education"

In K-12 education, the ability to use artificial intelligence (AI) to power adaptive learning has already allowed significant progress in how classes, teachers, and students interact. This technology has improved private schools and universities, and is quickly becoming more accepted in public classrooms across the country. Not only is AI-Powered adaptive learning seen as an effective way to provide learners with personalized instruction, but also a means to foster collaboration and active participation in the classroom.

First, we need to define what is meant by AI-Powered Adaptive Learning. By leveraging the power of AI, adaptive learning uses data to individualize instruction and to tailor content or resources to the individual student's needs and learning styles. With this technology, a computer algorithm is used to identify a student's strengths and weaknesses and offer a curriculum that is tailored to match their learning goals. The goal of this technology is to accelerate learning and increase student engagement.

AI-Powered Adaptive Learning also provides teachers with valuable analytics to track and monitor a student's progress as well as provide assessments and diagnostics. Through AI-Powered Adaptive Learning these tools can be used to personalize learning both in and out of the classroom. They provide teachers with the ability to quickly identify and address student's areas of weakness, provide additional instruction or resources to help them progress, or adjust curriculum to ensure that students are on track to meet the required learning outcomes.

By providing personalized learning for each student, AI-Powered Adaptive Learning also allows for greater collaboration in the classroom. Using AI-Powered Adaptive Learning tools, teachers can break down class groups into smaller units and assign tasks and challenges to the groups. This allows students to work together as they would in a typical classroom setting, while still receiving the benefits of personalized instruction. Through the use of AI-Powered Adaptive Learning tools, teachers can create an engaging learning environment that allows for collaboration and creativity while still keeping the students on track with personalized instruction.

AI-Powered Adaptive Learning also has the potential to help close the achievement gap between different demographics. The ability to provide personalized instruction, both in and out of the classroom, ensures that no student is left behind. Additionally, because AI-Powered Adaptive Learning relies on data collected from student performance, it can identify disparities in performance and allow the educational system to address these gaps.

There is the potential to revolutionize how K-12 classrooms operate. AI-Powered Adaptive Learning will not only provide personalized learning, but it will help teachers effectively monitor and track progress, further facilitate collaboration, and provide a platform for better assessment. The technology is already implemented in many private and university educational systems, and is quickly becoming more accepted in public classrooms across the country. As this technology becomes more advanced, more and more classrooms will be able to take advantage of its potential to revolutionize the way education is received.

Don't miss out!

Visit the website below and you can sign up to receive emails whenever Adam Smith publishes a new book. There's no charge and no obligation.

https://books2read.com/r/B-A-OSAW-WVTJC

BOOKS 2 READ

Connecting independent readers to independent writers.

Also by Adam Smith

AI in K-12 Education

Intelligent Machines in the Classroom: Unlocking the Potential of AI in K12 Education

Unleashing the Potential of Artificial Intelligence in K-12 Education: Reimagining How Learning Happens

Breaking Down Bad Habits

Breaking Down Bad Habits: How to Overcome Self-Defeating Behaviors and Achieve Success

Standalone

Brain Dead: When It Comes To Improving Mental Health, What The Hell Are We Waiting For?

40 Things Intelligent People Do Daily

The Beginner's Guide to Quantum Computing & Mechanics

Open Source AI

Watch for more at https://books2read.com/adamsmith.

About the Author

Adam Smith is a native North Texas Entrepreneur, social media expert, and educator who graduated from Embry Riddle University with a Bachelor of Science in Aerospace Studies. In 2007 he co-founded TeacherTube.com, an online education platform community that provides an educationally focused, safe venue for teachers, schools, and home learners. Under his leadership, in September of 2017, a publicly traded company, Salem Media Group, acquired TeacherTube. At the time of acquisition, TeacherTube had over 2 million registered educators with over 12 million monthly unique views of the site.

After the acquisition, Adam continued his passion for technology and education by helping schools and start-ups to large corporations with online training, branding, content marketing, and social media management.

To find out more about Adam, go to: https://books2read.com/adamsmith

Read more at https://books2read.com/adamsmith.

A. SMITH
MEDIA
Publishing Division | Texas

About the Publisher

A. Smith Media is a fully integrated digital media and distribution company specializing in producing and marketing television, film, home entertainment, music, and interactive games. A. Smith Media has been at the forefront of the commercial growth of Digital Distribution and Internet Video on Demand services through its pioneering efforts in web TV.

www.ingramcontent.com/pod-product-compliance
Lightning Source LLC
LaVergne TN
LVHW022024200926
848481LV00007B/2529